Speak Now

OR FOREVER HOLD YOUR

Speech!

HOW TO BECOME AN IRRESISTIBLE & PAID SPEAKER

BY: ERIKA TALIA MCCARTHY

MySpeakersBoutique.com

This book is dedicated to my amazing son.
I am constantly in awe of you and you are my best friend
and greatest teacher.

You are my victory child and I thank God for you every day.

You are the most intelligent, funniest, and sweetest child I know.
You're a natural leader and a firework, don't ever lose that.

I hope I've been a great example for you and I've been able to
show you that you can do anything your heart desires.

Follow the light and you'll overcome any darkness.

I love you more than the sun, the moon, and the stars.

XOXO,
Mommy.

About
THE AUTHOR
Erika Talia McCarthy

Erika Talia McCarthy is passionate about helping public speakers, entrepreneurs, coaches, and authors book paid public speaking engagements and podcast guest appearances to help them transform lives and grow and
scale their businesses.

Additionally, Erika is an authenticity, spirituality, mindset, and business coach who is passionate about assisting female entrepreneurs in establishing and expanding prosperous companies.

Erika received a bachelor's degree from Georgia State University and received her NLP, Life Coaching, and Business Coaching certifications as a result of understanding before you can start a successful business you must transform your mindset. Once your mindset is transformed your life and business will follow.

Erika is passionate about teaching others to incorporate spirituality and a limitless mindset into their goals and empowering others to be their truest and most authentic selves. She also loves helping women start a business they love without overworking and burning out! Erika is also a mom of an amazing 6-year-old son, a Disney fanatic, loves to travel, enjoys sewing, and long walks in nature.

Don't HAVE TIME TO APPLY FOR GIGS?

DONE-FOR-YOU PUBLIC SPEAKING SERVICE!
LET ME HELP YOU GET ON MORE STAGES!

SCHEDULE A CALL

MySpeakersBoutique.com
hello@myspeakersboutique.com

©Copyright 2023
by My Speakers Boutique, LLC

Disclaimer:

No part of this book, eBook, or audiobook may be reproduced in any form without permission in writing from the author.

The book, eBook, and audiobook are for entertainment purposes only and are not a guarantee of a successful business, income or specific amount of income, or a specific number or type of public speaking engagements or podcast interviews.

This is not a replacement for professional advice from your business coach, life coach, attorney, bookkeeper, accountant, or any other professional you hire. Discretion is advised. The author can not be held responsible for any loss, claim, or damage arising out of the use, or misuse of what is written in this book, eBook, and audiobook.
Always seek professional advice.

Use of any techniques outlined in this book, eBook, and audiobook is the personal responsibility of the reader and not the author or publisher.

No part of this book, eBook, or audiobook may be duplicated, distributed, transmitted, reproduced, or sold in any form without permission in writing from the author.

By law, only the author or publisher, who is the owner of the copyright, has the right to reproduce or distribute the book, eBook, and audiobook, unless express permission has been granted.

Under no circumstances will any blame or legal responsibility be held against the publisher, or author, for any damages, reparation, or monetary loss due to the information contained within this book, eBook, and audiobook. Either directly or indirectly.

Legal Notice:

This book is copyright protected. This book is only for personal use. You cannot amend, distribute, sell, use, quote or paraphrase any part, or the content within this book, without the consent of the author or publisher.

Images from Canva.com

WHY I'M PASSIONATE ABOUT HELPING YOU BOOK MORE SPEAKING GIGS!

& Testimonials

SCAN WITH THE CAMERA ON YOUR PHONE

Watch The Video

Book A Call

https://bit.ly/publicspeakersletschat

How To Land Speaking Gigs...

Even If You're Just Getting Started

VISIT OUR WEBSITE

MYSPEAKERSBOUTIQUE.COM
HELLO@MYSPEAKERSBOUTIQUE.COM

Find Your Next Speaking Engagement

SPEAKING DATABASE

WANT ACCESS TO MY PUBLIC SPEAKING DATABASE WITH 1000S OF EVENTS THAT NEED SPEAKERS & MY VIDEO TRAINING PORTAL WHERE I TEACH YOU HOW TO BOOK SPEAKING ENGAGEMENTS?

- 1200 Events currently in database for 2023 and 2024.
- Easily Search by event type *(virtual or in-person)*, location, application deadline, industry, etc.)
- Training portal with step-by-step videos that teach you how to book engagements.

SCAN TO PREVIEW THE DATABASE

PAY & GAIN ACCESS TO THE DATABASE

Visit My Etsy Shop For More Public Speaking Resources!

https://www.etsy.com/shop/MySpeakersBoutique

Chapters

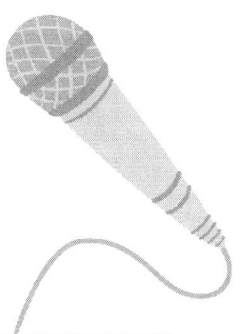

Chapter 1 - Life Is A Gift, Don't Waste It!

Chapter 2 - It's Not Just A Speech!

Chapter 3 - The Power of Public Speaking Unveiled!

Chapter 4 - The Power of Your Why!

Chapter 5 - Discipline Can Make or Break You!

Chapter 6 - Why Your Business Is Suffering.

Chapter 7 - Skyrocket Your Business Using Your Voice!

Chapter 8 - Ways To Increase Your Income In The Next 60-90 Days!

Chapter 9 - You Need Help & I'm Here To Be Of Service!

Chapter 10 - Ready To Find Speaking Gigs? Here's How!

Chapter 11 - Crafting a Winning Speakers Proposal!

Chapter 12 - Don't Be Shy, Brag On Yourself!

Chapters

Chapter 13 - Set Your Speaking Business Up For Success!

Chapter 14 - How To Stand Out To Event Planners!

Chapter 15 - How To Get Booked And Paid As A Speaker!

Chapter 16 - New To Speaking? You Can Still Book Gigs!

Chapter 17 - Thank You!

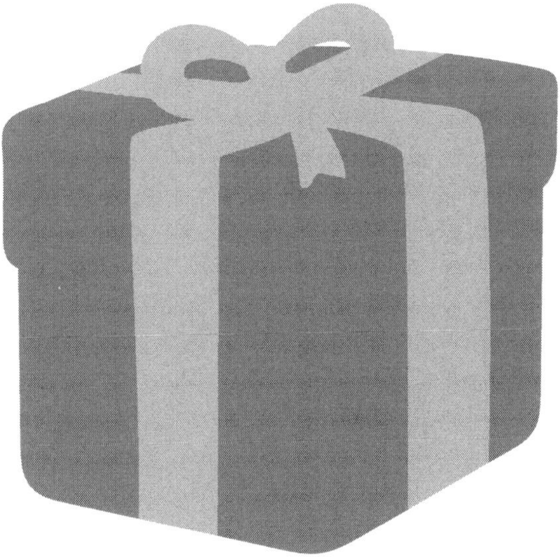

Chapter 1
Life Is A Gift, Don't Waste It!

God gave us the gift of life; it is up to us to give ourselves the gift of living well. - Voltaire

Public speakers completely transformed my life!
When you're on stage, please remember, it's not just a speech!

I woke up in the middle of the night some years ago with the worst chest pain I'd ever experienced! I couldn't breathe, my chest felt like someone was deliberately squeezing like a stress/pressure ball due to how uncomfortably tight it was, and I was fairly certain I was suffering a heart attack.

The problem was, I was in my mid 20's, and having a heart attack at that age was simply unimaginable!

When they say, "Your life flashes before your eyes" they are speaking pure truth. I began to pray, I asked God to save me and make the pain go away, then I began to think about my family, friends, and those closest to me. I would miss them terribly and I didn't even get to say
"Goodbye" or "I love you".

I wasn't a mom at the time, but I wanted to be one, so I imagined the child I would never have.

Well, my fears did not win, because now I have the most amazing son and beautiful gift from God, (I call him my victory baby for this very reason).

You don't realize how much you take life for granted and how much you take your health for granted until death is staring you right in your face.

Have you ever seen Death? It can be very scary if you're not prepared.

I was in gut-wrenching pain, yet, I was also suddenly heartbroken. I knew I had so much more to do with my life, so many more goals to reach, and a bigger purpose, and I was literally heartbroken that I didn't take action to make my dreams a reality sooner.

It's true, we don't know our time or our place and oftentimes we live life as though we are invincible.

As I was being raced through the streets on what felt like the longest journey of my life, screaming out in pain, I was hit with a harsh reality check that reminded me that I was far from invincible.

We live life as though we have all the time in the world, and my prayer for everyone reading this book is you live the longest, most blessed, happiest, and healthiest life you can possibly imagine, however, I am your witness that your life can change forever and permanently in the blink of an eye.

If you are able to pursue your dreams and goals today or more specifically your public speaking career, do it <u>now</u>! Don't procrastinate, and hush all of those voices that will tell you 1000 reasons why you can't and shouldn't go after your dreams.

I know what regret feels like when you think you've met up with your final day on Earth in this life and trust me, the sting of regret is worse than the pain I felt when I thought I was having a heart attack.

You don't want to feel the permanent sting of regret, trust me!

Write the book now, apply for those speaking engagements now, start the business now, go back to school now, be the best parent and/or spouse you can be now, ask for that promotion now, travel to that country now, ask for or give forgiveness now, tell that person you love them now, apologize now, take a leap of faith now... now, now, now!

This life God has given us is a beautiful gift but it doesn't last forever, whatever mark or legacy you are meant to leave in this world is something only you can provide, now.

I personally feel as though I owe it to God, my ancestors and Spirit, my son, myself, my family, my community, and the world to stop holding myself back and boldly go after my dreams.

Studies say there is about a 1 in 400 trillion chance of you being born, if that is not a miracle, I don't know what is!

You won the victory and beat out about 400 trillion others when you were born, how dare you let fear hold you back! Do you realize what faith, strength, determination, and boldness it took for you to get here?

Starting right now, there are no more excuses.

We can't totally eliminate fear, but we can replace the actions that fear produces.

Fear produces stagnancy, procrastination, and excuses. Starting now, you can decide to retrain your mind and say moving forward when you feel fear (and you will) it will now produce faith, courage, determination, consistency, and the mindset that you are going to go after your dreams anyway.

Allow fear to make you unstoppable, not stagnant.

You can't eliminate fear, but you can change the actions you take after you experience fear.

As a reminder, fear is not necessarily bad, and in many situations such as when you're in danger, fear can save your life as fear's job is to protect you. So we don't want to completely eliminate fear.

However, fear is also notorious for popping up anytime we make the slightest change. Why? Because our brains, our mind, and our fears naturally don't care too much for change, we are creatures of habit, so change can pose a threat to our mental and emotional psyche.

However, as I'm sure you've experienced change can be good, right?

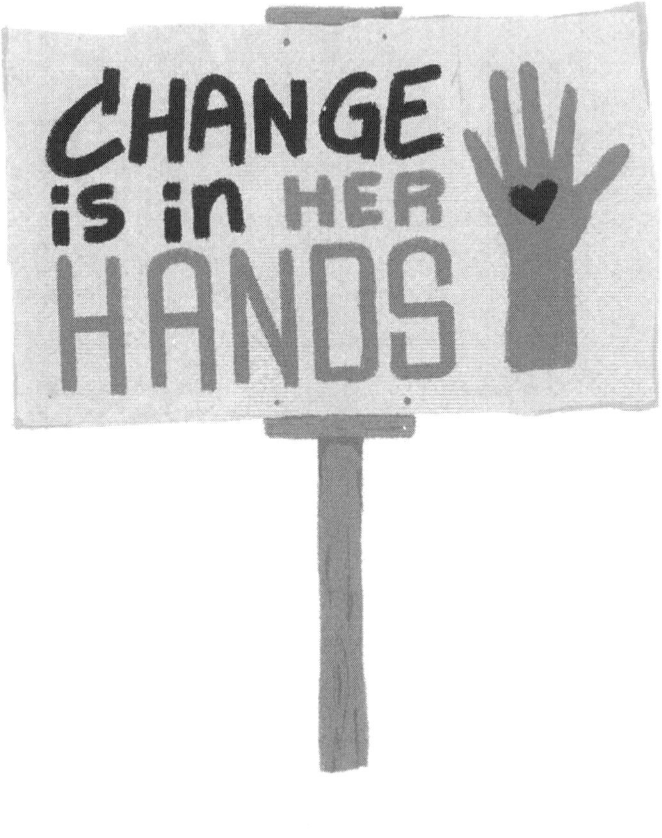
CHANGE
is in HER
HANDS

- When you decided to move to a better neighborhood, that was a good change!

- When you decided to finish school and get your degree, that was a good change.

- Listening to God's voice when He said "That is your wife" or "That is your husband", after you've been single for years, was a good change

- Making the decision to not give up on your business no matter how many times you have to try and try again, was a good change.

- Making the decision to put your kids in the best schools, homeschool them, or provide a top-notch education for them, was a good change.

- Hiring that assistant so you can stop burning yourself out and stressing, was a good change.

- Eating healthier, exercising, and making your mental, spiritual, emotional, and physical health a priority, was a good change.

As you can see, you are an expert at navigating and being victorious as you're experiencing change!

Deciding to become a public speaker, become a highly paid public speaker, and take your business and speaking business to the next level is just one more change that you will triumph over!

Just so you can see how many amazing choices and changes you've personally made in your life, on the next couple of pages, I want you to list changes you've experienced and how you triumphed over those changes!

I'm a Master At Change!

Here is how I've personally triumphed over change in my life!

WAYS I TRIUMPHED OVER CHANGE

I'm a Master At Change!

Here is how I've personally triumphed over change in my life!

WAYS I TRIUMPHED OVER CHANGE

As you see, change can be good, so from this day forward, you will not take this precious life you have for granted, and you will embrace change and go after your dreams, right?

Okay, now that we've mastered fear and change let's continue with the story.

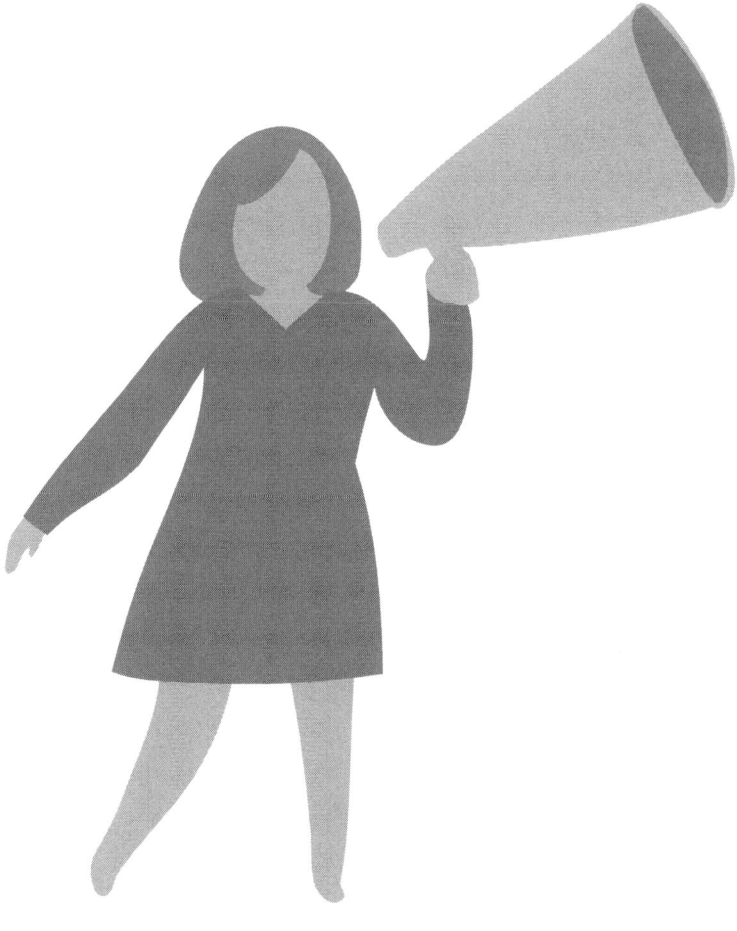

Chapter 2
It's Not Just A Speech!

"They may forget what you said, but they will never forget how you made them feel." - Carl W. Buechner

Have you ever had a doctor say,
"I'm sorry, I don't know what's wrong with you"?

I have!

I love doctors, nurses, and healthcare workers, without these amazing, selfless, and incredible people with huge hearts we would not be as healthy as we are and we would have lost so many lives.

If you are in the health and wellness field, whether you help people heal physically, mentally, emotionally, or spiritually, I want to thank you for your service and sacrifice. You are loved and needed.

Doctors are known to be experts but I realized even doctors can be baffled. This was a very unsettling feeling to say the least, because I was incredibly ill and my doctor had no idea what was wrong with me or even how to treat me to reduce or eliminate the symptoms.

As I lay in my hospital bed I was not only having a mental breakdown, drifting into a very deep depression, and experiencing dark thoughts, but I developed even more severe physical symptoms very suddenly.

I developed pneumonia, I developed even more chest pain, I developed huge rashes all over my body and face, extreme fatigue, dizziness, blurred vision, loss of memory, kidney issues, extreme fatigue, and the inability to walk... as in my muscles literally would not work and allow me to get out of bed and walk.

I was terrified, absolutely terrified.

During this time I also saw more doctors than I've ever seen in my life.

I saw several ER doctors, a cardiologist, an infectious disease doctor, an internal medicine doctor, a neurologist, a pathologist, a nephrologist, and there are probably others that I'm forgetting. The bottom line is I saw a ton of doctors but no one knew how to diagnose me.

<u>No one knew the name of my disease.</u>

Do you realize how important a name is?

- When you give your child a name, that name has meaning and that meaning stays with your child for the rest of his or her life.

- When someone remembers your name after briefly meeting you,
you feel honored.

- When someone prays for you or your loved ones, they say your name(s) to ask God to activate the healing specifically for you.

- The last name of your family lineage can make you a hero in your town or the family everyone wants to stay away from.

- When your name is called as the keynote speaker you feel a rush of adrenaline that instantly energizes you.

- When you can name your disease, you know how to heal it or at least treat it.

Hearing all of these highly intelligent, well-educated, doctors and health experts tell me they had no idea what was wrong with me released so many thoughts and feelings inside of me.

I was scared, I was confused, I was angry, I was lost, I was depressed, I was anxious, I was in pain, I was sad, I was losing my faith, I was stressed, I was and I felt unloved, unseen, and unheard.

I had a lot of family and friends around me who are still my rock and my support system to this day, I love them dearly, but somehow even their words of encouragement and comfort didn't help ease my pain.

If the doctors had no idea how to treat me or make me whole and feel better, who did?

GOD DID!

During this very dark and uncertain time in my life, I had two choices, I could either give up on life and sink or somehow muster the strength to hold my head above water for one more day and swim.

I <u>decided</u> to swim.

Since I couldn't get out of bed, I was very limited in the things I could do.

However, somehow, I had this inner knowing or gut feeling, that before I started to work on my physical well being I had to transform my mental well-being.

The thoughts of sickness, disease, pain, and doom and gloom were not helping me at all.

Yes, this was my physical reality, I was sick, in excruciating pain, with an un-named disease, however, my mind did not have to be a victim of mental disease as well.

Although my body was weak, I could make my mind even stronger as a way to compensate for what my body lacked at the time.

When they say "All you can do sometimes is pray", I am a witness that all you can literally do sometimes is pray!

I was a child that grew up in the church. My grandmother (Nana) is an ordained mister and a very powerful woman of God.

My mom kept my brother and me in church,
we were in the choir and I feel like my mom can quote bible scriptures and stories for days. She knows her Bible in and out and often quotes Bible stories and scriptures to me when I need encouragement.

I am surrounded by powerful spiritual leaders to this day including a wonderful woman I call my spiritual mother.

I am no stranger to church, however, I did not have a personal relationship with God at that time.

Church and reading my Bible was something I did because it was in my blood, it was something my family did, and I naturally followed in their footsteps.

However, in that hospital bed, and as I was released and readmitted to the hospital time and time again, I developed a personal and unbreakable relationship with God.

It wasn't enough to believe in God because Nana or my mom believed in God, it wasn't enough to call on the name of Jesus because they did,
I had to know Christ for myself.

My family's faith was not going to carry me over this mountain, I had to carry myself over the mountain by strengthening my faith and seeking a personal relationship with God.

I did just that.

I started with prayers, I had powerful and praying women all around me my entire life, from my great-grandmother who is still living and is currently 97 years old, to my Nana, and mom.

Prayer was not new, but before now it was something I was "supposed" to do.

I had never really said a deep prayer that was so vulnerable, powerful, authentic, and meaningful that I knew God was right there in the room with me.

I began to pray daily.

I picked up my Bible, and again, reading the Bible was not new, however, I had never taken time to study and digest the scriptures. Usually, I read the Bible because I was told to or because I felt it was something I just did, never because I actually wanted to study and seek healing, wisdom, and understanding.

My daily prayers and reading of the Bible daily completely transformed my life, and I experienced increased faith, spiritual and emotional healing, and a closer relationship with God.

However, I did not stop there.

I had this spark one day, I don't know how or where it came from I just know it happened suddenly and soon the spark grew into a wildfire that I could no longer ignore, I knew I needed to flow with the feelings and follow the guidance and downloads I was receiving.

I had this spark to start journaling. It also led me to start reading about the power of words, the Law of Attraction, and how to shift your mindset, along with only listening to positive messages.

Some may say this is extreme but with the state I was in, I knew I needed to at least try.

I began to develop a daily routine of ...
- Prayer
- Reading my Bible
- Writing in a gratitude journal daily
- Meditation
- Visualization
- Writing down my feelings
- Speaking affirmations out loud and writing them down in the form of I AM
- Learning about the power of the mind
- Learning about the Law of Attraction
- Learning how to manifest health and my dream life
- and Listening to preaching, public speakers, and leaders share their stories of faith and victory

I still do all of these things almost daily and they have most definitely become a part of my lifestyle!

I like to say **WORDS TRANSFORMED MY LIFE** because they most definitely did!

When I say that as a public speaker, you are not reciting speeches that are meaningless, you are literally transforming lives!

I am a witness to that!

WORDS ARE POWERFUL AND CAN TRANSFORM LIVES!

Preachers, public speakers, and authors helped to activate my healing and strengthen my faith when it was almost lost.

As a public speaker, you never know who is in the audience or in a hospital bed on the other side of headphones listening to your story and words. You don't know whose life you are saving.

My family and friends helped me so much during this very difficult time, from my mom and brother driving me to the hospital and doctors appointments, to helping me with chores around the house, to calling and checking on me, to my childhood friend/sister making me vegan meals, to Nana, Papa, and my other family and friends praying for me and sending gifts.

My loved ones were my rock, but I like to say, God, Jesus, public speakers, and authors were my strength.

I had nothing else to lean on when I was lonely and in pain in my bed with tears streaming down my face, except prayer, my Bible, and the words of public speakers and authors like yourself.

I had to make a determination to change my thoughts, my words, and my mindset, my family and friends could not do that for me.

Making positive changes mentally, allowed me to make positive changes physically. For example, after extensive research, I decided to try out a vegan lifestyle during this time. I read so many positive things about how veganism helped to heal many people's diseases, and I felt I had nothing left to lose, so I gave it a try.

Before you make changes to your diet, exercise plan, or lifestyle please consult your doctor, spiritual leader, nutritionist, personal trainer, and/or therapist.

Developing these healthy habits not only allowed me to think more positively and strengthen my faith mentally and spiritually but they helped to improve my emotional and physical wellbeing.

I began to feel better and look healthier and I was able to walk and eventually run and exercise!

Also, after countless hospital and doctor visits, blood work, and tests, a wonderful Rhumotoligst was able to name my disease.

I was diagnosed with Systemic Lupus Erythematosus (SLE) or Lupus for short.

Although I was in no way, shape, or form happy about being diagnosed with a chronic, autoimmune disease, I was relieved I could finally name the disease.

This helped my Rheumatologist and me develop a plan of action to keep my symptoms to a minimum.

They say you can not cure Lupus, you just learn to manage the symptoms the best way you can, however, I am a living testimony that you can still live a "normal" life despite being diagnosed with the disease.

My Rheumatologist has been in awe over the years at how well I am able to manage my symptoms, he says I am one of the few patients whom he can barely even tell I've been diagnosed with Lupus except when he does my bloodwork... those words are music to my ears!

I attribute my miraculous "silent" Lupus symptoms to my relationship with God, believing that when Jesus died on the cross, I was already healed, and this Bible verse which my mom recites to me often,

"But He was wounded for our transgressions, He was bruised for our iniquities; The chastisement for our peace was upon Him, And by His stripes, we are healed." - Isaiah 53:5

and my lifestyle change of journaling, positive affirmations, listening to positive messages, exercising (now I take walks outside several days a week and I joined kickboxing and aerial silk rope/lyra hoop classes), and changing my diet (I am now mostly plant-based and pescatarian on some days, however, I do my best to still eat a very healthy diet with a few cheat days here and there).

All of these things along with the tremendous support of my family, friends, loved ones, and co-workers at the time who were incredibly kind and even threw me a "Welcome Back" party when I returned to work and bought me a cute little stuffed animal named, Lupie,
helped me completely transform my life.

Do you remember when I told you change can be very good? Well, I am your example of how positive changes, and triumphing over your fears can literally heal and transform your life and the lives of others.

As a public speaker, you are a doctor of words and you help people see the small glimmer of light when all they can see is darkness.

Whether you are helping someone heal, teaching them a business or marketing technique, saving a family or marriage, or motivating them to reach their goals and not give up on their dreams, you are transforming lives.

It is time for you to **Speak Now Or Forever Hold Your Speech** because someone out there is waiting just for you!

Studies Show

"Word of mouth can affect sales figures up to 5 times more than traditional means of advertising." -CreativeQuills.co.uk

A neuroscience experiment called "Do Words Hurt" proved negative words release stress and anxiety-inducing hormones. - BRM Institute

"A single word has the power to influence the expression of genes that regulate physical and emotional stress." - Dr. Andrew Newberg

Own your POWER

Chapter 3
The Power of Public Speaking Unveiled

"Find out what's keeping them up nights and offer hope. Your theme must be an answer to their fears."
- Gerald C Myers

Public speakers are more important now than ever! In an era defined by social media and the ability to connect to others easier than ever, the ability to communicate clearly and effectively has become more crucial than ever before.

As we've discussed in the previous chapters, captivating TED Talks that inspire change to mesmerizing keynote addresses that rally masses, the ability to deliver a compelling message has the potential to transform lives and shape the course of history.

Through countless hours of research, interviews with renowned speakers, and personal experiences on stage, I have gained invaluable insights into the nuances of effective communication and how to find and book public speaking engagements.

In this book, I'd love to present this knowledge and share it with you, as my goal is to help you bring your public speaking dreams to life!

Whether you are an introvert searching for the confidence to command a room, an executive seeking to elevate your leadership presence, or a student eager to excel in presentations, this book will serve as your guide.

Embark on this transformative journey with me as we unlock the secrets to becoming an exceptional public speaker. Let us shatter the barriers that hold us back, embrace the power of our words, and step into the spotlight with conviction.

Together, we will elevate the way we communicate and make a lasting impact on the world around us.

I'M AN IRRESISTIBLE SPEAKER!

I want you to repeat this over and over again until you feel you're an irresistible and unforgettable speaker with every fiber of your being!

Becoming a dynamic and irresistible public speaker does take faith, time, dedication, consistency, and the willingness to master the art of speaking, however, if you were not meant to share your story, knowledge, and wisdom with the world you wouldn't have a desire to speak. Period!

Someone, somewhere NEEDS the information you have to share!

Someone, somewhere is waiting for you to have the courage to share your voice!

Someone, somewhere needs to connect with you on stage, at a virtual summit, during a podcast interview, or read your article.

They are waiting for YOU!

I know it's gut-wrenching to think about getting on stage in front of a ton of people to deliver a speech that they may love, like just slightly, or even despise.

However, it's important to remember that we're often our own worse critics.

You may think your speech isn't good enough, you may think your voice sounds weird, you may think everyone is staring at the pimple that broke out on your forehead the day before your big engagement, you may think your outfit looks hideous, however, most people don't even notice these things, or if they do, it's not their main focus. even if everyone in the audience doesn't resonate with your speech, your goal is to change and touch at least one life.

The power of one is real and it works!

When you're starting out on your speaking journey or even if you've already done a ton of speaking engagements, remember the **POWER OF ONE!**

You see my friend, even if everyone in the audience doesn't resonate with your speech, your goal is to change and touch at least one life. The power of one is real and it works! If one person claps, if one person comes up to you afterward and tells you about a breakthrough they received, if one person says they want you to speak at a future event, if one person says they are glad they came to the event, then you've done your job!

Think about transforming one life at a time, not winning over all 100 people in the room.

Someone in the room will complain about your speech, outfit, voice, (FILL IN THE BLANK)

just know chances are you'll have at least one critic, but we all do!

It's sort of like going to the movies and seeing the hottest, new thriller. 95% of people can rave about the movie, tell their family and friends to see it, and even go back to the theatre to see the movie a second time.

However, we all know someone, somewhere will absolutely despise the movie, right?

They will say the theme music didn't go with a certain scene, or they picked the wrong leading actress, or the movie was filmed in the wrong city.

Trust me, there's a critic for everything. When we speak, our natural tendency is to focus on who won't like us or who will think we're a horrible speaker, this is natural, most of us do it.

However, I'd like to encourage you to shift your mindset, my friend, don't focus on who won't appreciate the knowledge you shared, don't focus on who will have something negative to say, and instead zero in on the fact that you have a **RAVING FAN** somewhere in the audience and your job is to help them receive an aha moment, transformation, or breakthrough.

Your raving fan won't care that your tie isn't the exact hue of blue as your pants.

Your raving fan won't care that you had to clear your throat five times because you were nervous.

Your raving fan won't care that you sweated through your shirt, your raving fan won't care you paused a bit too long because you forgot what you were going to say.

Your raving fan will know and recognize that you're an **IRRESISTIBLE** speaker and they will be thrilled you showed up! If you won't show up for yourself, show up for your **RAVING FAN!**

transformation

I AM IRRESISTIBLE!

WRITE DOWN 3 AHA MOMENTS, TRANSFORMATIONS, OR BREAKTHROUGHS
YOUR AUDIENCE WILL RECEIVE AFTER HEARING YOU SPEAK

TRANSFORMATION 1

AHA MOMENT
-
-
-
-

TRANSFORMATION 2

AHA MOMENT
-
-
-
-

TRANSFORMATION 3

AHA MOMENT
-
-
-
-

MORE TRANSFORMATIONS

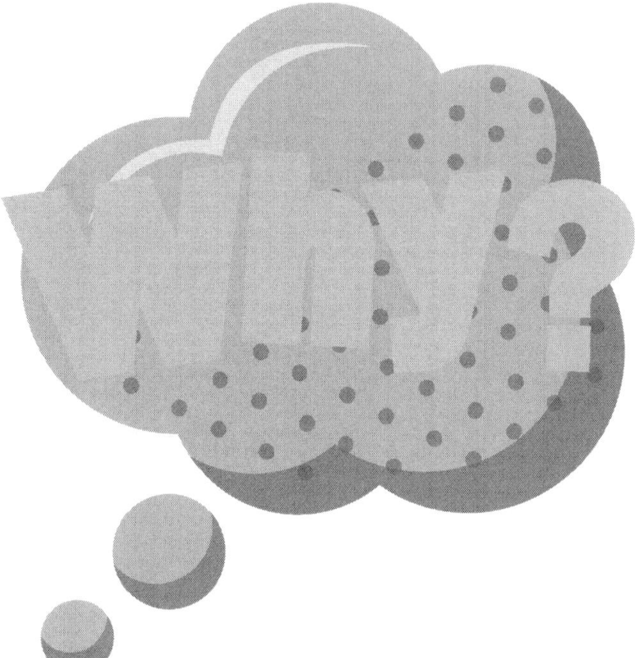
WHY?

Chapter 4
The Power of Your Why!

"Before we can stand out, we must first get clear on what we stand for." — Simon Sinek

What is your **WHY** and **WHAT** do you stand for?

Before you can develop a successful speaking career you must know why you want to speak. Speaking just to make money, sell books, or enroll people in your high-ticket coaching programs may work and bring in some income for a while however, the glory days may last for a while, however, your spark may quickly ware off without a solid **WHY**.

Yes, as a public speaker it's important to sell books, services, and get paid, however, public speaking is so much more than that! Do you want to be a public speaker that helps people overcome health issues, or save their marriages, or encourages them to start the business they've always wanted to start?

Have you overcome childhood trauma, poverty, or negative self-talk, and could you help people overcome these things as well?

Put yourself in the shoes of your audience members. What are they struggling with? What answers and keys do you have that can help others?

Do you wish to deliver the next "I Have a Dream" speech or Theodore Roosevelt's "The Man in the Arena"?

Is your ultimate goal to leave a legacy for your family or transform so many lives you help future generations?

What is your **WHY?** Make sure your why is strong enough to help you to keep going when you want to give up because there will be times when you want to give up. Your why must keep you going!

On the next page, write down what your **WHY** is and how your **WHY** will help you keep going when you want to quit and transform lives when you're on stage.

this is my why

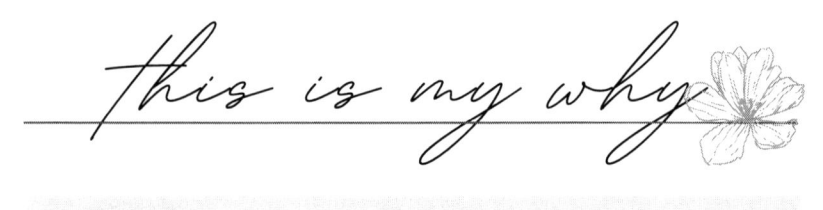

this is my why

this is my why

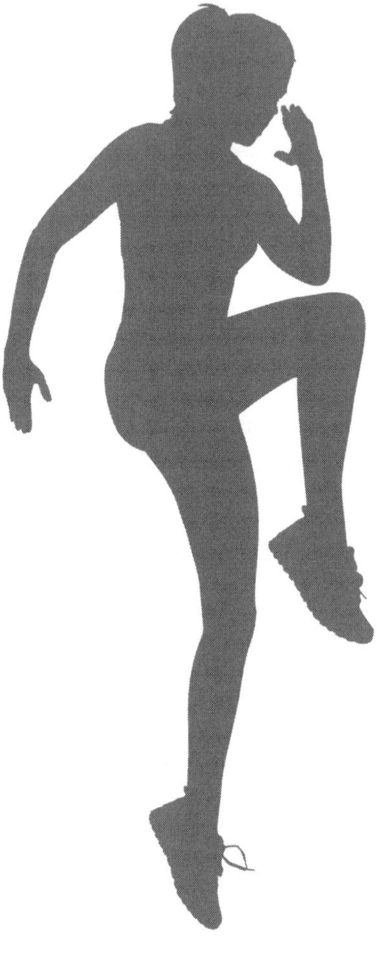

Chapter 5
Discipline Can Make or Break You!

"Discipline is the bridge between goals and accomplishment." - Jim Rohn

As you start building your speaking career, discipline will be critical to your success.

Until you become a well-known speaker you're doing to have to be consistent at building your speaking business, applying for engagements, following up, and positioning yourself as an irresistible speaker.

Set a goal now to be so disciplined with pitching yourself to speaking gigs that it will eventually become second nature to you. Remember, there are a ton of speakers who want to speak at the same events as you do.

If you only apply to one speaking engagement per month, it's not impossible, but it's highly unlikely that you'll build a successful speaking career.

There will be a lot of hard, tedious work that you'll need to put into pitching yourself for engagements in the beginning, however, if you're diligent enough you'll eventually start to receive emails and phone calls asking you to speak, yay!

Do the hard work in the beginning and you'll see how much it will pay off later in your

Create an action plan and stick to it!

Sometimes you will deviate from your action plan, don't worry, we all do! If you have an off day just get back on course the next day.

You'll feel amazing, accomplished, and like you're making excellent progress in your speaking career if you stick to your plan.

Yes, the most exciting part for most public speakers is actually transforming lives from the stage, however, in order to get to the stage, you must do the boring, tedious tasks. You'll feel like quitting if you don't get a **YES** in the first few weeks, or even after a few months, however, please don't give up on your dreams, the **YES** will come. You got this, my friend!

HERE ARE EXAMPLES OF HOW YOU CAN CREATE A DISCIPLINED AND LUCRATIVE SPEAKING CAREER

- I will exercise, eat well, and get plenty of rest!
- I will devote 30 minutes daily to practicing my speech and stage presence!
- I will hire a communication coach!
- I will apply to 10 speaking engagements per day!
- I'll listen to 30 minutes of motivational content daily to uplevel my mindset!
- I'll spend 30 minutes watching others give speeches and learning about public speaking daily!
- I will schedule 30 minutes per day for myself for self-care and self-love!
- One weekend a month will be my "Go hard or go home day". This is the weekend where you spend 4-8 hours pitching, filling out applications, etc.!
- I will create business cards displaying I'm a speaker and give them to everyone I meet!
- I will follow up with event planners I haven't heard back from every 2-3 days!
- I spend 30 minutes a day making connections with event planners.
- I will make sure my social media reflects my speaking expertise.
- I will attend one networking or speaking event a month, tell the attendees I'm a public speaker, and hand out my business cards.

Here Are Examples of Business Cards You Can Create

- You can create business cards on VistaPrint.com, Staples.com, and Canva.com to name a few.

- Virtual Business Cards with a QR code can be scanned via a phone. The QR code can lead to your website.

- Physical business cards can be ordered and shipped quickly or in some cases picked up within 24 hours.

- Always have your business cards on you!

Discipline = Success!

SETTING YOUR GOALS

SET YOUR SPEAKING GOALS FOR THE NEXT 30, 60, AND 90 DAYS

ACTION PLAN — 30 DAYS
-
-
-
-

ACTION PLAN — 60 DAYS
-
-
-
-

ACTION PLAN — 90 DAYS
-
-
-
-

Discipline = Success!

SETTING YOUR GOALS

SET YOUR SPEAKING GOALS FOR THE NEXT 30, 60, AND 90 DAYS

30 DAYS ....

ACTION PLAN
- ○
- ○
- ○
- ○

60 DAYS ....

ACTION PLAN
- ○
- ○
- ○
- ○

90 DAYS ....

ACTION PLAN
- ○
- ○
- ○
- ○

Discipline = Success!

SETTING YOUR GOALS

SET YOUR SPEAKING GOALS FOR THE NEXT 30, 60, AND 90 DAYS

30 DAYS ....

ACTION PLAN
- ○
- ○
- ○
- ○

60 DAYS ....

ACTION PLAN
- ○
- ○
- ○
- ○

90 DAYS ....

ACTION PLAN
- ○
- ○
- ○
- ○

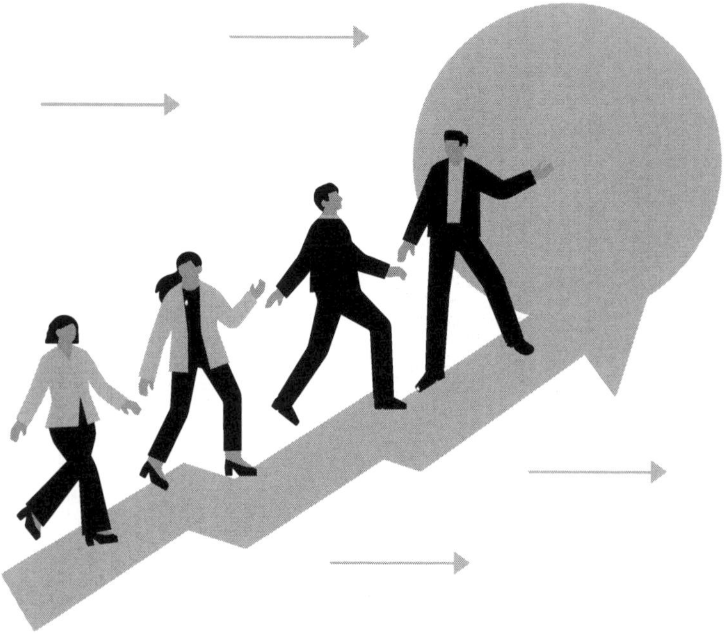

Chapter 6
Why Your Business Is Suffering!

"There's no shortage of remarkable ideas, what's missing is the will to execute them." - Seth Godin

Your public speaking business IS **NOT** suffering because you're not smart enough, good enough, you don't work hard enough, or you aren't meant to be a business owner.

Your business is suffering because you simply need the tools, resources, the right dream team, systems, and most importantly the mindset to take your business from mediocre to your **DREAM BUSINESS.**

I **KNOW** You Can Create The Business of Your Dreams And.... if you don't believe it yet, I'm here to help you see the vision.

As your Public Speaking Booking Agent, I am not only here to help you book public speaking engagements, podcast interviews, run your ads, or help you create your digital course.

I'm also here to help you show you that you're meant to transform lives with the power of your voice and that your message is meant to be heard by thousands if not millions of people around the world. **NOW IS THE TIME** to share your message - not tomorrow, not a year from now, but **NOW!**

<u>I'm sure you've seen these stats</u>

- 20% of new businesses fail during the first two years of being open
- 45% during the first five years
- 65% during the first 10 years
- Only 25% of new businesses make it to 15 years or more!

Those stats are alarming, I know, but with the right mindset, team, resources, and tools you and your business will be a part of the elite 25% of businesses that make it 15 years or more!

Okay, so now that we know how many businesses fail, it's important to learn **WHY** they fail so we can do our best to avoid those problems, right?

Why Businesses Fail

Financial Hurdles → Inadequate Management → Failing To Leverage Future Growth → Marketing Mishaps

Now that we know the reasons why businesses fail, allow me to show you how public speaking and partnering with me as your Public Speaking Booking Agent can help you overcome and avoid these obstacles.

Why Your Business Will Succeed!

Financial Hurdles

It takes income to run a business. Furthermore, it takes healthy financial habits to sustain your business.

If you want to grow and scale, you need to increase your sales, period.

How I Will Help

Public Speaking (virtual or in-person), being a guest on podcasts, creating a digital course, and running ads are all great ways to not only increase sales but to help you increase brand awareness which leads to organic traffic and sales.

Inadequate Management

If you don't have the right team, systems, and SOPs (Standard Operating Procedures) in place to grow your business it's a recipe for disaster.

Furthermore, if you're trying to do everything yourself in your business it leads to burnout and eventually you quitting.

How I Will Help

As your Public Speaking Booking Agent, I am happy to take tasks off of your plate so you can focus on other things in your business. I will not only reach out to events, companies, and people on your behalf I will handle all of the administrative tasks from start to finish.

Failing to Leverage Future Growth

Starting a business is great! Writing a book is wonderful! Putting up your website is fantastic!

However, if you're not thinking about ways to grow your business and leverage future growth, your business will quickly become stagnant.

How I Will Help

As your Public Speaking Booking Agent, I will help your business grow by leveraging new and creative ways to market your business. Writing a book is great but selling it is event better!

Marketing Mishaps

Marketing is everything in business. Effective and efficient marketing can be the difference between your business skyrocketing or falling flat.

When you get your marketing efforts right, your business soars!

How I Will Help

As your Public Speaking Booking Agent, I will help you create a fun and effective marketing outreach campaign which can include public speaking (virtual or in-person), podcast guest appearances, digital course creation, ads and more!

Chapter 7

Skyrocket Your Business Using Your Voice!

"The human voice is the organ of the soul."
-Henry Wadsworth Longfellow

In this chapter, we will explore the numerous reasons why you should consider becoming a public speaker and how it can positively impact your life.

Amplify Your Voice:

Public speaking provides a platform for your ideas, experiences, and expertise to be heard by a larger audience. As a public speaker, you have the opportunity to share your knowledge and insights, inspire others, and create positive change. Whether you're addressing a small group or a large audience, your words have the power to influence and motivate people.

Develop Confidence and Leadership Skills:

Becoming a proficient public speaker requires practice, self-reflection, and continuous improvement. As you gain experience and refine your speaking abilities, your confidence will grow. Overcoming the fear of public speaking can be a major personal victory, boosting your self-esteem and providing a sense of achievement.

Additionally, public speaking nurtures leadership skills. It teaches you how to command attention, engage with diverse audiences, and convey your message persuasively. These skills are transferable to various aspects of life, including professional settings, community engagements, and personal relationships.

Expand Your Network:

Public speaking engagements offer valuable networking opportunities. By sharing your ideas and expertise on a public platform, you can connect with like-minded individuals, industry professionals, and potential collaborators. Attending conferences, seminars, and events related to your speaking topics can further broaden your network and open doors to new possibilities.

Influence and Inspire Others:

Public speakers have the power to influence people's perspectives, beliefs, and actions. By sharing your stories, knowledge, and passion, you can inspire others to think differently, challenge societal norms, and take action towards positive change. Your words have the potential to touch hearts, transform lives, and create a ripple effect that extends far beyond the speaking engagement itself.

Personal Growth and Continuous Learning:

Becoming a public speaker is an ongoing journey of personal growth and self-improvement. Each speaking engagement offers an opportunity to learn from the audience, receive feedback, and refine your communication skills. Public speaking pushes you to research, stay informed, and develop expertise in your chosen topics. It encourages you to step outside your comfort zone, embrace new challenges, and keep expanding your knowledge and horizons.

Career Advancement:

Public speaking can significantly enhance your professional prospects. It establishes you as an authority in your field, increasing your visibility and credibility. Many industries value effective communicators, and being a skilled public speaker can set you apart from your peers. It can lead to invitations for speaking engagements, media appearances, consulting opportunities, and even book deals. Public speaking can become a key differentiator in a competitive job market and help you advance your career to new heights.

WHY YOU SHOULD BECOME A PUBLIC SPEAKER!

Although we are focused on public speaking engagements in this book, public speaking doesn't have to mean you getting on stage and talking to a bunch of people if that's not your cup of tea.

There are so many ways to share your message including...

Virtual Public Speaking Engagements Podcast Guest Appearances
Creating a Digital Course
Teaching Others
Running Ads and Marketing Your YouTube Channel
Book
Course
Social Media Accounts

The great news is my team and I specialize in all of the above!

Public Speaking can...

- Help you establish yourself as an expert in your field
- Build your confidence and skill set
- Set yourself apart from the competition or help you stand out in a competitive niche
- Increase your visibility and brand awareness online and offline
- Save time - Instead of coaching one person you'll coach many people at once
- Make more appointments and close more deals
- Sell your books faster
- Increase your network

INCREASE YOUR INCOME

Chapter 8
Ways To Increase Your Income In The Next 60-90 Days!

"It is not the economy that determines your income, it is your own personal development"
—*Mac Duke The Strategist*

Let us take a second to evaluate the most common revenue streams for speakers and how speakers like yourself can incorporate more revenue streams to quickly increase income.

MOST COMMON REVENUE STREAMS FOR SPEAKERS

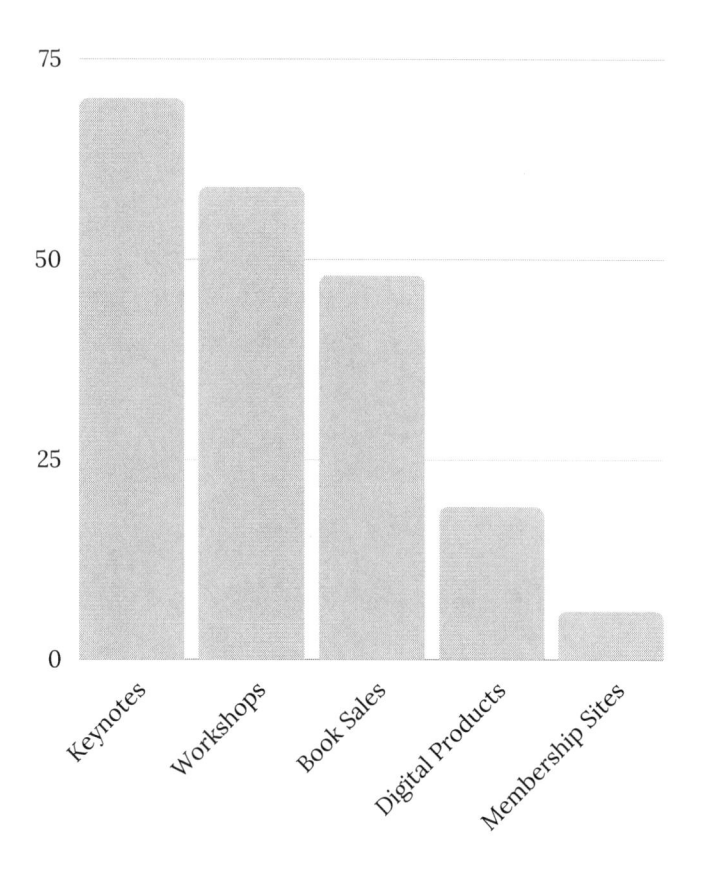

As you can see most speakers rely on Keynotes and Workshops to generate the majority of their revenue. However, book sales, digital products like digital courses and eBooks, and membership sites are highly under-utilized.

Did you know, the average "Professional" Public Speaker earns about $106,000 per year?

However, non-speaking activities account for an incredible 60% of the speaker's income!

Selling books, online courses, coaching & consulting sessions, webinars, etc. are the bulk of the speaker's total income.

What does this mean for you?

IF YOU'RE NOT PROMOTING YOUR BOOK, ONLINE COURSE, COACHING/CONSULTING PACKAGE, OR WEBINAR,
YOU'RE LOSING MONEY!

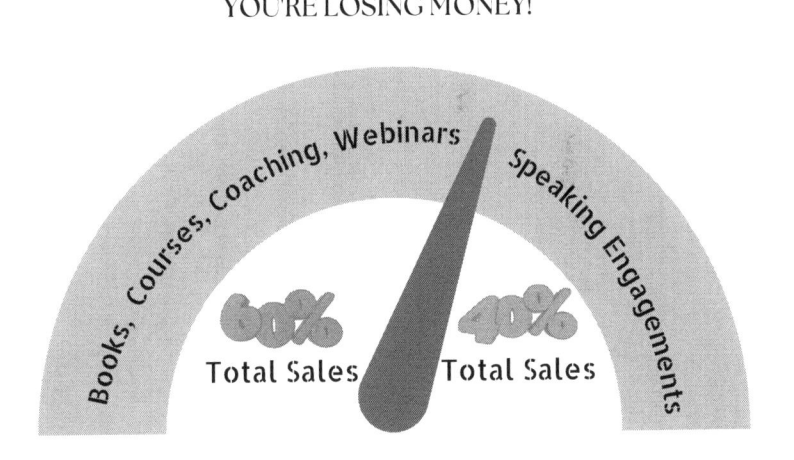

Why You Need Digital Products

Whether you're an author, coach, public speaker, consultant, or influencer digital products can help you create passive revenue streams that generate money for you in your sleep.

Have you ever thought about turning passages of your book into an eBook that gives your social media followers and email subscribers a sneak peek before they buy?

Have you thought about giving your audience a chance to join your subscription service or video training after hearing your speech?

What about turning your book into an Audiobook or full Digital Course or Membership Site?

Digital Products can and will create passive income for you and give you creative ways to leverage your already existing books, speeches, coaching resources, social media posts and videos, etc.

Turn Your Resources Into Cash!

Here are just a few digital products you can create with your books, coaching resources, social media posts, blog posts, newsletters, articles, and more!

- Ebooks
- YouTube Videos
- Audiobooks
- Email Courses
- Workbooks
- Audio Trainings
- Video Trainings
- Master Classes
- Online Stores
- Mastermind Groups
- Online Courses
- Membership Sites
- Subscription Services
- Licenses Giving Companies Permission to Use
- Your Training Materials

Turn Your Resources In Cash!

Do you see how powerful the digital product ideas listed above can be for your business?

Here's the issue with the *old* way of doing things.

Public Speaking generates income which is great, but you only make income for one speech at a time.

Book sales can be slow and it can take a while for your book to generate consistent revenue.

Coaching sessions rely on your physically being there which takes up time, energy, and resources. You can't be in two places at once so coaching puts a cap on the amount of revenue you can generate.

DIGITAL PRODUCTS CREATE PASSIVE INCOME, FOREVER, WHILE YOU SLEEP!

Are you pinching yourself and asking why you didn't create a digital product sooner yet?

How Can I Be of Service?

I'm here to be of service to you and help you...

- Get booked in virtual or in-person stages as a Public Speaker.

- Increase your email subscribers, social media following, and book and course sales via podcast interviews.

- Run your paid ads so you can sit back, relax, and watch your business grow.

AND

I want to help you do so much more than that!

I also want to help you create your eBook, digital course, membership site, audio training, YouTube videos, text message campaigns, and so much more which can help you skyrocket your business and create passive and residual income!

With my proven methods, you can start generating more revenue in as little as 60-90 days!

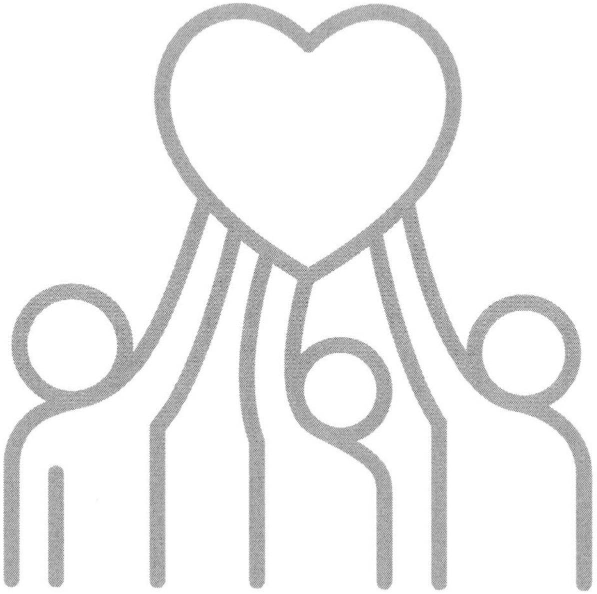

Chapter 9

You Need Help & I'm Here To Be Of Service

"Service to others is the rent you pay for your room here on earth."
- Mohammed Ali

Which Category Do You Fall Into?

49% of Speakers, Authors, and Business Owners say Sales makes them nervous.

32% say Marketing makes them anxious.

18% Say Operations makes them nervous.

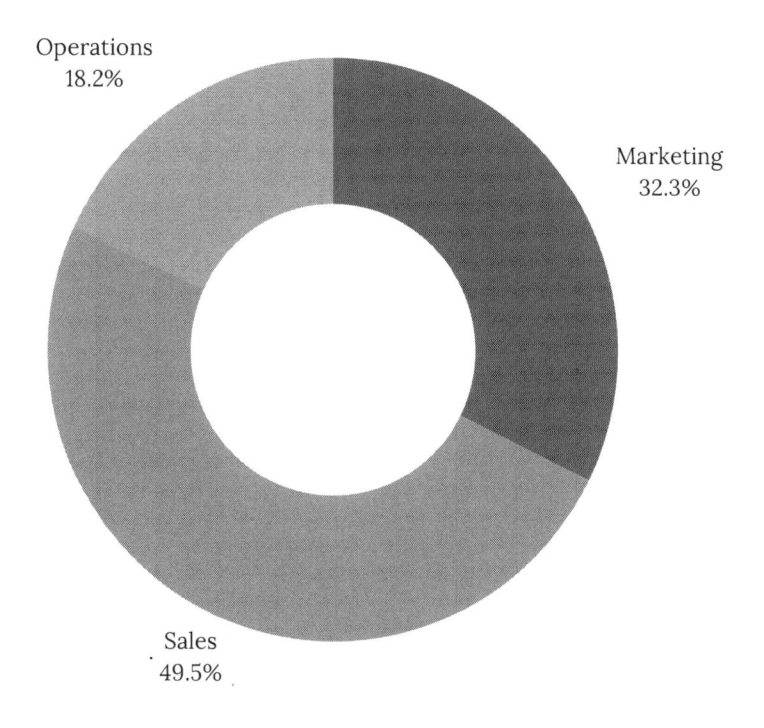

- Operations 18.2%
- Marketing 32.3%
- Sales 49.5%

To summarize a whopping **82%** of leaders like yourself say revenue-generating activities make them nervous, can you relate?

If so, I'm here to help ease your anxiety by taking some of your time consuming activities off of your plate!

"Do what you do best and outsource the rest."
-Peter Drucker

HERE'S WHY YOU SHOULD PARTNER WITH ME

83% of Public Speakers don't prospect for new speaking gigs. 83% say prospecting is the hardest part of their business.

NO WORRIES! I DO ALL THE PROSPECTING FOR YOU!

I am a skilled and professional Speaker's Agent and Marketing Agent who can take the behind-the-scenes tasks off of your plate so you can focus on what you do best, speaking and transforming lives!

Wouldn't life be so much easier if you can just show up to your event and hand all of the other tasks off to someone else?

Well, that someone else is me!

I'm Super Excited to be your new speaker's agent and I can't wait to help you make more money and gain a ton of your time!

I'm Here To Help!

Email me at **hello@myspeakersboutique.com** to get started.

OR SCAN THE CODE TO TELL ME MORE ABOUT YOUR PROJECT!

https://bit.ly/publicspeakersletschat

I can't wait to partner with you!

Erika Talia McCarthy

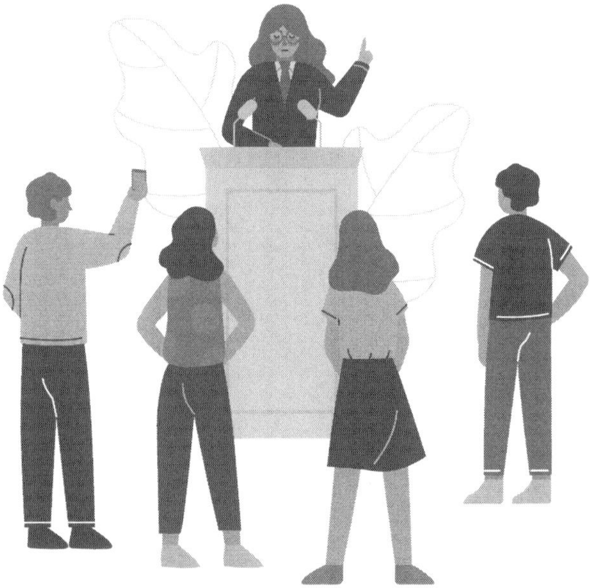

Chapter 10
Ready To Find Speaking Gigs? Here's How!

"Always give a speech that you would like to hear."
- Andrii Sedniev

Public speaking opportunities are everywhere!

You can get booked as a public speaker from the unlikeliest places, however, actually getting booked and paid as a public speaker takes persistence and time.

Researching and finding public speaking opportunities requires a proactive and strategic approach. Begin by defining your target audience and the topics you excel in. Utilize search engines, industry-specific directories, and event listing websites to discover conferences, seminars, workshops, and organizations relevant to your expertise. Join professional associations and networks, attend industry events, and connect with event organizers and fellow speakers to expand your knowledge of upcoming opportunities. Engage with social media platforms, such as LinkedIn and Twitter, to follow relevant hashtags, join industry-specific groups, and stay updated on industry trends. Additionally, consider reaching out to local community organizations, universities, and professional development programs, as they often seek speakers for their events. Regularly monitor event calendars, sign up for newsletters, and leverage personal connections to tap into the hidden gems of public speaking engagements. Remember, persistence and a proactive mindset are key to unearthing a wealth of speaking opportunities

Researching and finding public speaking opportunities is a crucial step towards establishing yourself as a speaker and sharing your expertise with the world. In this chapter, we will explore effective strategies and techniques to uncover a wide range of speaking engagements that align with your target audience and areas of expertise. By adopting a proactive and comprehensive approach to research, you will maximize your chances of securing meaningful opportunities and reaching your speaking goals.

Define Your Target Audience and Expertise:

Identify your target audience: Determine the demographics, interests, and needs of the audience you wish to reach with your message.
Determine your areas of expertise: Clearly define the topics you excel in and are passionate about sharing with others.

Utilize Online Resources Like The Ones Listed:

Search engines: Use search engines like Google to find conferences, seminars, and events related to your field of expertise. Include specific keywords, such as "call for speakers" or "speaker opportunities," to narrow down your search.

Event listing websites: Explore dedicated event listing platforms like Eventbrite, Meetup, or 10Times.com, industry-specific directories to discover upcoming events and speaking opportunities.

Industry associations and directories: Join relevant professional associations and access their directories to find conferences and organizations that cater to your target audience.

Networking and Industry Connections:
Attend industry events: Participate in conferences, trade shows, and networking events within your industry to connect with event organizers and fellow speakers. Building relationships can lead to future speaking invitations.

Social media engagement: Utilize platforms like LinkedIn, Instagram, and Facebook to follow industry influencers, join relevant groups, and engage in discussions. Networking online can lead to valuable connections and awareness of speaking opportunities. You can also find upcoming events on these platforms.

Connect with event organizers: Proactively reach out to event organizers, introduce yourself as a speaker, and express your interest in speaking at their events. Leverage your network to seek introductions or request recommendations. You can also provide event organizers with something of value such an event planning checklist to help them organize their events.

Local Community Organizations and Educational Institutions:

Community organizations: Research local chambers of commerce, nonprofit organizations, and community groups that regularly host events. Reach out to them to inquire about speaking opportunities relevant to your expertise.

Universities and educational institutions: Contact universities, colleges, and professional development programs to explore possibilities for guest lectures, workshops, or panel discussions. Remember each college has different departments so verify you're reaching out to the correct department and person.

Industry Publications and Newsletters:
Industry-specific publications: Keep an eye on trade magazines, blogs, and online publications within your field. Some publications may feature articles or interviews that highlight speaking opportunities.

Event newsletters: Subscribe to newsletters of event organizers, industry associations, and online communities to receive updates on upcoming events and speaking opportunities.

Hidden Gems and Personal Connections:

Tap into personal connections: Reach out to colleagues, mentors, friends, and acquaintances who may have information about speaking opportunities or be able to provide introductions.

Local networking groups: Investigate local business networking groups, clubs, and professional organizations that may host regular events where speakers are needed.
Conclusion:

Researching and finding public speaking opportunities requires a multifaceted approach that combines online research, networking, industry engagement, and leveraging personal connections.

By defining your target audience, utilizing online resources, building networks, exploring local organizations, staying informed through industry publications, and tapping into personal connections, you will unlock a vast array of speaking engagements tailored to your expertise.

Embrace a proactive mindset and maintain persistence as you navigate the world of public speaking, and watch as doors open to exciting opportunities to share your message and make a lasting impact.

HERE ARE MORE WAYS TO FIND SPEAKING ENGAGEMENTS

- Universities
- LinkedIn Groups
- LinkedIn Events
- GigSalad.com
- NsaSpeaker.org
- Facebook Groups
- Facebook Events
- Chambers of Commerce
- GlobalSpeakersFederation.net (Intl. Events)
- Speakersforschools.org
- Churches
- Podcasts
- Eventbrite.com
- www.AssociationExecs.com
- Meetup.com
- www.Talkwalker.com/alerts
- Corporations (Inc 500, 1000, 5000)
- www.SpeakerMatch.com
- Digital.gov/events
- CharityNavigator.org
- Speaking Databases

Find Your Next Speaking Engagement

SPEAKING DATABASE

WANT ACCESS TO MY PUBLIC SPEAKING DATABASE WITH 1000S OF EVENTS THAT NEED SPEAKERS & MY VIDEO TRAINING PORTAL WHERE I TEACH YOU HOW TO BOOK SPEAKING ENGAGEMENTS?

- 1200 Events currently in database for 2023 and 2024.

- Easily Search by event type *(virtual or in-person), location, application deadline, industry, etc.)*

- Training portal with step-by-step videos that teach you how to book engagements.

SCAN TO PREVIEW THE DATABASE

PAY & GAIN ACCESS TO THE DATABASE

How Will Find Your Next Gig?

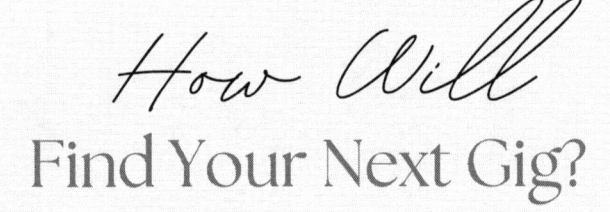

Write down what you'll do to find your next speaking gig?

I WILL FIND MY NEXT GIG BY

How Will Find Your Next Gig?

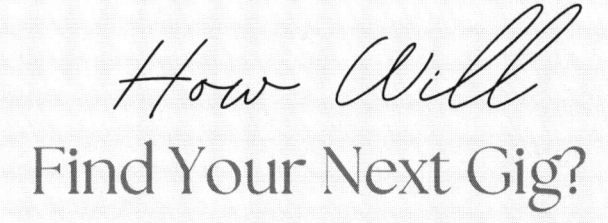

Write down what you'll do to find your next speaking gig?

I WILL FIND MY NEXT GIG BY

Chapter 11

Crafting A Winning Speakers Proposal

"Either write something worth reading or do something worth writing."
--Benjamin Franklin

Becoming a world-class public speaker is very possible and I believe in you!

However we must recognize that highly sought-after speakers are not developed overnight, it takes strategy, grit, and time.

One strategy that helps you stand out among other speakers as you're applying for speaking engagements and making connections with event planners and leaders, is a winning speaking proposal.

You will send each event your speaking proposal to showcase why they should select you as their keynote or breakout speaker.

Crafting a winning speaker proposal is an essential skill that can set you apart in the competitive world of public speaking.

Begin by creating a captivating bio that showcases your expertise, credentials, and unique experiences, capturing the attention of event organizers.

Next, craft an impactful topic description that clearly communicates the value and relevance of your presentation to the target audience, addressing their pain points and offering solutions.

Supporting materials such as previous speaking engagements, testimonials, and multimedia content can further bolster your proposal and provide evidence of your speaking prowess. Tailor your proposal to each specific event, demonstrating a thorough understanding of the organizer's objectives and audience demographics. Furthermore, tailor your speaking topic titles to each event as well.

By combining a compelling bio, an engaging topic description, and relevant supporting materials, you will increase your chances of crafting a winning speaker proposal that stands out and positions you as the ideal candidate for the speaking engagement.

Don't forget a call-to-action and follow-ups.

Many speakers miss out on their opportunity to speak and get paid because they do not include a call to action.

After you finish applying for that speaking engagement or DMing, emailing, or calling the event planner invite them to have another phone call with you if all details weren't finalized on the first call, or invite them to have a Zoom call with you so you can learn more about the event and audience and to also showcase your areas of expertise and explain why you would be the best fit as their speaker.

I've gotten so many of my speakers booked and paid for speaking events by simply inviting the event organizer to chat with me further via phone or Zoom.

Please don't forget a call-to-action, this can literally be the difference between a YES and a NO.

Additionally, if you've submitted a speaking application, or emailed, called, or DMed the event organizer and you haven't received a reply, please follow up with them every 2 to 3 days.

Event organizers are busy so it may be that they wanted to reply but forgot, so don't take their silence as a NO.

Again, I've secured my speakers and myself for different speaking engagements by simply following up with the event organizers. If an event organizer asks you to email them again in a week, please do so, this is a clear sign that they may be interested in having you speak, they may just be a bit busy at the moment.

A CRM like Hubspot, Leadific, and so many more can help you add in reminders and stay organized regarding who to follow up with and when. A CRM also allows to you capture important information that you may want to remember such as notes during the initial phone call, how much the event can pay speakers, and application deadlines.

Things don't stop once you follow up with the event organizer a few times or get booked as their speaker. It is incredibly important to continue to nurture the relationship with that event organizer and other event planners as well.

Understanding the importance of networking and cultivating relationships with event organizers, industry professionals, and fellow public speakers is crucial for advancing your public speaking career.

Networking provides opportunities to connect with key decision-makers, learn from experienced speakers, and stay informed about industry trends. Both online and offline networking techniques are essential to expand your reach.

Offline, attending industry events, conferences, and meetups allows you to interact with professionals face-to-face, exchange insights, and build personal connections.

Online networking, on the other hand, enables you to connect with a global audience through social media platforms like LinkedIn, Facebook, and Instagram and professional forums.

By actively engaging with industry professionals, participating in discussions, and sharing valuable content, you can establish your expertise and attract speaking opportunities.

Some ways to connect with event organizers would be to like and comment on posts, congratulate them in the DMs when they receive a promotion, or say "Happy Birthday" when you see a birthday notification for them,

Embrace networking as a powerful tool to cultivate relationships, gain visibility, and unlock a world of possibilities for your public speaking career.

Chapter 12
Don't Be Shy, Brag On Yourself!

"It's an essential exchange in the world of work-to be seen and heard and to see others."
— Lisa Bragg

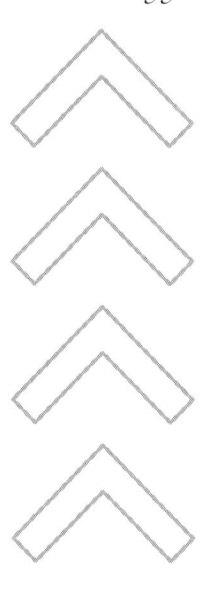

Showcasing your speaking skills is essential for building credibility and attracting future speaking engagements.

Take advantage of various platforms and opportunities to demonstrate your expertise.

Local meetups, Toastmasters clubs, and similar community gatherings provide supportive environments where you can refine your skills, receive feedback, and gain confidence in front of an audience.

Online speaking contests offer a wider reach and the chance to compete against other speakers while gaining exposure. You can then use these contests to showcase your speaking ability and book speaking engagements.

Additionally, video recordings of your presentations are invaluable assets that allow potential organizers to witness your stage presence, delivery style, and ability to engage an audience.

Aim for high-quality recordings that capture the essence of your speaking prowess.

Testimonials from previous event organizers, attendees, or clients further enhance your credibility, highlighting the impact you've made as a speaker. Simply ask for a quick 60-second video testimonial or written testimonial.

Embrace these opportunities to showcase your speaking skills, leveraging videos and testimonials as powerful tools to convince and inspire others to invite you to speak at their events.

Another great way to easily collect amazing testimonials is a program I love called Talkadot.

Talkadot is a survey and a great way to collect testimonials all in one!

Talkadot allows you to add a QR code to the end of your presentation slides and when audience members scan the QR code they can quickly take a survey to highlight what they loved about your speech and leave a written testimonial for you.

You'll receive a report with feedback that you can share on social media or send to other event planners.

Furthermore, if an audience member needs a speaker for one of their upcoming events there is an easy way to indicate they want you to speak at their next event while submitting the survey.

Yay! Isn't this incredible?

This is an easy way to easily collect leads for future upcoming events and almost get guaranteed bookings for future paid speaking events!

You can also collect reviews after you do podcast interviews, for book launches and more!

READY TO SEE TALKADOT IN ACTION? SCAN THE CODE!

Give feedback to Erika

1. Scan this QR code

2. Enter this code on the screen

200OFF

or go to talk.ac/myspeakersboutique   Powered By talkadot

Want $200 Off My Speaking Database With 1000s of Events Who Need Speakers?
You'll Also Gain Access To My Video Training Portal Where I Teach You How To Book Events And Get Paid!

Enter 200OFF When The Screen Asks You To Enter A Code

TalkaDot In Action!

These are examples of reports you'll receive once someone fills out a survey after hearing you talk.

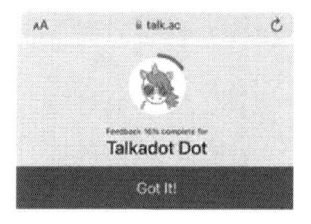

Was Talkadot's talk valuable for you today?

Yes

No

Was Talkadot's talk actionable?

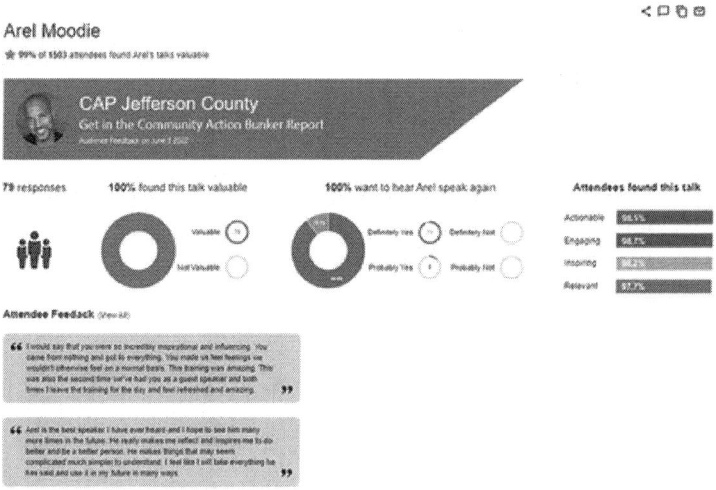

Arel Moodie

⭐ 99% of 1503 attendees found Arel's talks valuable

CAP Jefferson County
Get in the Community Action Bunker Report
Audience Feedback on June 3 2022

79 responses | 100% found this talk valuable | 100% want to hear Arel speak again

Valuable / Not Valuable
Definitely Yes / Definitely Not / Probably Yes / Probably Not

Attendees found this talk
- Actionable 98.5%
- Engaging 98.7%
- Inspiring 98.2%
- Relevant 97.7%

Attendee Feedback (View All)

" I would say that you were so incredibly inspirational and influencing. You came from nothing and put in everything. You made us feel feelings we wouldn't otherwise feel on a normal basis. This training was amazing. This was also the second time we've had you as a guest speaker and both times I leave the training for the day and feel refreshed and amazing. "

" Arel is the best speaker I have ever heard and I hope to see him many more times in the future. He really makes me reflect and inspires me to do better and be a better person. He makes things that may seem complicated much simpler to understand. I feel like I will take everything he has said and use it in my future in many ways. "

Want Your Own TalkaDot Code?
Scan Below!

talkadot

Use the Free Version
OR
Get a 30 Day Trial of the Paid Pro Version

https://app.talkadot.com/referrer?via=myspeakersboutique

SUCCESS

Chapter 13

Set Your Speaking Business Up For Success

"You cannot manage what you cannot measure"
Peter Drucker

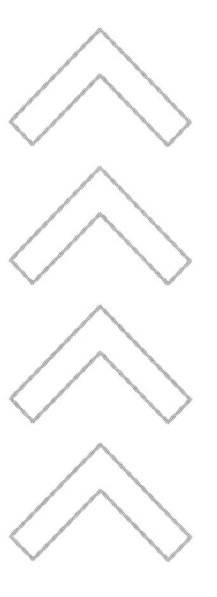

In today's fast-paced and highly competitive business landscape, effectively managing and organizing your business and customer relationships is crucial for success.

There are many tools and systems you can use in your public speaking business to keep things organized.

This is where Customer Relationship Management (CRM) systems, along with other integrated business systems, come into play.

A CRM system allows you to centralize and streamline your customer data, interactions, and communication, providing a comprehensive view of your customers and their preferences.

It enables you to track leads, manage sales pipelines, nurture relationships, and provide personalized experiences.

Additionally, integrating other systems, such as marketing automation, project management, and accounting, can further enhance your operational efficiency and productivity.

By implementing these systems, you can optimize your processes, improve collaboration, enhance customer service, and make informed business decisions based on accurate and up-to-date data.

Ultimately, having a robust CRM and other integrated systems empowers your business to cultivate strong customer relationships, streamline operations, and drive growth in a competitive marketplace.

I personally love HubSpot and Leadific as CRM tools to help me organize conversations with event planners and keep track of important dates such as application deadlines and when to follow up about certain events. Additionally having a bookkeeper or using QuickBooks can help you send invoices and organize payments received from speaking gigs and expenses.

I love Asana, Trello, and ClickUp as project management tools to organize my day-to-day tasks such as making 20 connections with event planners and larger projects such as finishing a book or completing the slide deck for a speaking gig.

Tools like Buffer can help you remain consistent and active on social media since you can schedule posts. This will keep you top of mind and also show event planners you're serious about your speaking career since you are consistent on social media. Use social media as a tool to highlight your expertise and talk about your speaking
topics.

You should also create a speaker's bio/one sheet or media kit, speaking video reel, and a speaking website that highlights your speaking topics, books you've written, awards, past speaking engagements and podcast interviews, media features, testimonials, what transformations the audience will receive, and your speaking fees if you wish to list them.

Your website can also have a page specifically for event planners which lists why they should hire you, how you stand out from other speakers, and how they can book you to speak.

Additionally, as I mentioned in a previous chapter think about having a free offer that s valuable for your audience and creating an opt-in page to collect names, emails, and phone numbers if they give you permission to do so. This free offer can help you grow your email list. You can create a free offer for event planners and one for audience members at your events that way you can simultaneously grow an email list of planners who need speakers and of audience members who need your products and services.

Finally, many speakers make additional income from promoting or selling their products or service at events. Your entire speech should definitely not be a sales pitch, however, mentioning your offer at the end of your talk if the event allows can help you sign more clients, or sell more products or books. Additionally, you can ask for a table to be set up in the room to display your products and services, and/or you can ask the event to purchase bulk copies of your books.

Helpful Tools

- CRM (Leadific, HubSpot)
- Speaking One Sheet
- Speaking Video Reel
- Speaking Website
- Title of Presentation
- Description of Presentation
- 3 Takeaways the Audience Will Recieve
- Free Offer/Lead Magnet
- Paid Offer (i.e. Book, Course, Coaching, etc.)
- Way To Collect Testimonials (i.e. Talkadot)
- Ways to create presentation slides (Canva or PowerPoint)
- Speaking contract (You can download one online from a reputable website, a lawyer can create one for you, or visit my Etsy shop to download one)

Visit My Etsy Shop For More Public Speaking Resources!

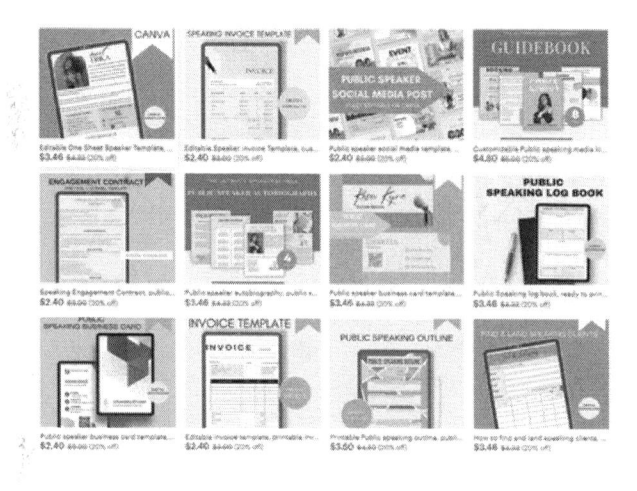

https://www.etsy.com/shop/MySpeakersBoutique

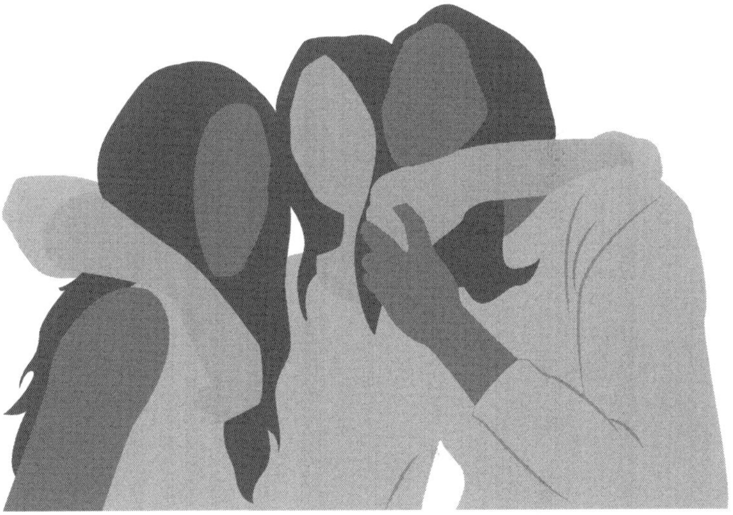

Chapter 14

How To Stand Out To Event Planners!

"We Do Not Remember Days We Remember Moments." - Cesare Pavese

When event planners are selecting public speakers, they have specific criteria in mind to ensure the success of their events and the satisfaction of their attendees.

First and foremost, event planners seek speakers who possess expertise and knowledge in a particular subject matter, as this ensures that the content delivered is valuable, informative, and relevant.

Additionally, event planners look for speakers who can engage and captivate the audience, delivering their message with charisma, enthusiasm, and authenticity.

Strong communication skills, the ability to connect with diverse audiences, and a dynamic stage presence are highly valued attributes.

Event planners also consider a speaker's reputation and track record, looking for individuals with a proven ability to deliver impactful presentations and leave a lasting impression.

Flexibility, professionalism, and the capacity to tailor content to the specific needs and goals of the event are also essential. Finally, event planners often prioritize speakers who are easy to work with, responsive to communication, and committed to delivering a seamless experience for both the organizer and the attendees.

By embodying these qualities, public speakers increase their chances of being selected by event planners and making a significant impact on the success of the event.

Really taking the time to customize your speaking topics and speaking titles is also another great way to stand out to event planners.

Many public speakers copy and paste the same topics and titles and they do not take the time to craft a specific talk for each event. Yes, it can be time-consuming to write a specific proposal and talk for each event, however, you'll quickly stand out as the event planner can tell you did not just copy and paste your proposal. Take time to really research the event and audience then write three specific ways that you can deliver a transformation and breakthrough.

I suggest creating about three different speaking titles and topic descriptions to start, you can use these talks and outlines as templates but please make sure you customize your email or speaking proposal after learning more about the event or audience.

Other Ways To Stand Out

- Send a free offer (i.e. eBook, PDF copy of book, event planner magazine, access to one training video in course, 15-minute consultation, webinar)

- Mail copies of your book to events you aren't speaking at. This helps you land more client-partners and keeps you top of mind the next time an event planner needs a speaker.

- Send a DM on Facebook or LinkedIn for birthdays, anniversaries, and job promotions.

- Send Christmas or holiday eCards.

- Create customized videos for LinkedIn introductions for schools, corporate offices and events, you can talk specifically about the value you will bring to their event in the video.

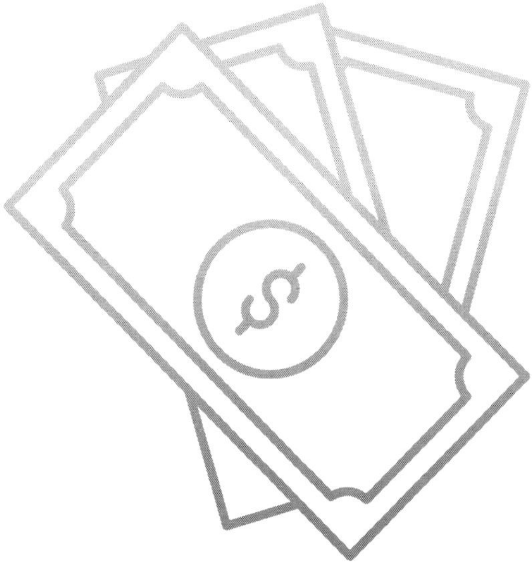

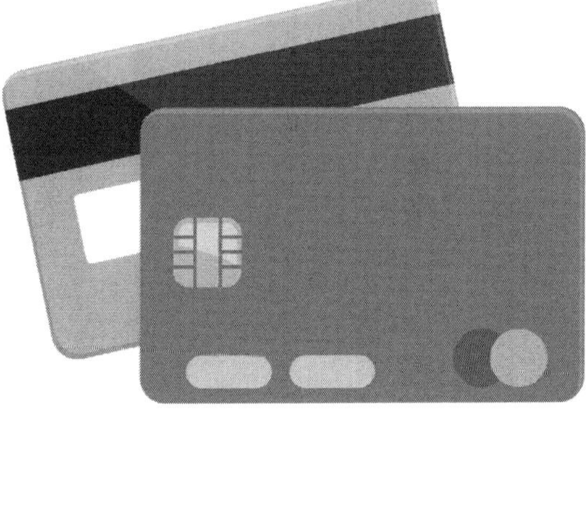

Chapter 15

How To Get Booked And Paid As A Speaker!

"Speaking for Free Gets You A Fee"
- Erika Talia McCarthy

Repeat after me- "*I deserve to be paid well for the value I bring.*"

As an expert in your field and a transformer of lives, you absolutely deserve to get paid for your ability to transform lives and businesses.

When you go to a doctor, you pay!
When you see a therapist, you pay!
When you hire a business coach, you pay!
When you enroll in college courses, you pay!

If you pay to receive healing, expert knowledge, and business advice, why shouldn't you get paid to do the same thing for other people?

As a public speaker, it is important to recognize and assert the value of your expertise and the time and effort you invest in preparing and delivering presentations.

Requesting payment for your speaking services is not only reasonable but also necessary to sustain your speaking career.

By asking to get paid, you are acknowledging the professional nature of your work and the value you bring to events and audiences.

Compensation demonstrates that your expertise is highly sought after and recognizes the years of experience, research, and honing of your craft that have led you to the stage.

Additionally, receiving payment allows you to dedicate more time and resources to continuously improving your skills, developing new content, and expanding your reach as a speaker.

By valuing your worth and seeking compensation, you are not only contributing to your own success but also upholding the standards of the speaking industry as a whole.

What To Think About
WHEN NEGOTIATING YOUR FEE

- The type of event you want to speak at. For example, you may ask corporations for a different fee than non-profits due to their prospective budgets.

- Can this engagement turn into more than a speaking event? Can you promote coaching sessions or license out your products?

- How many times you've spoken before? You can negotiate higher fees the more times you've spoken.

- Response from event planners (i.e. are they saying your fee is too high or low?)

- Look on other speakers' websites and see how much they charged to speak at that conference. This will give you an idea of that conference's budget.

- Speaking goals for the year (i.e. goal is to make $20,000 from speaking and you want to speak at 5 events, you should ask for $4,000 per event).

How To
NEGOTIATE YOUR FEE

According to Foundr.com here are some guidelines to consider when negotiating your fee. This is not a rule set in stone, please negotiate the fee that feels best for you while considering the type of event, number of audience members, budget for the event, travel distance, etc.

- Fewer than three talks: $500 – $2,500 per talk

- 3 – 8 talks/proven expert/first-time author: $5,000 – $10,000 per talk

- 8 – 12 talks/micro-influencer (5K-100K followers)/multiple books: $10,000-$20,000 per talk

- 12+ talks/social media influencer (100K+ followers)/bestselling author – $20,000 – $35,000 per talk

There are times when it may be beneficial to speak pro bono or for free.

For example, the event may be a virtual event and you'll have an opportunity to share your products and services during the event, or if you're attending an in-person event, the networking opportunities and the people who will be in the room would be worth you speaking pro bono to make a connection with those people. or maybe the event is for a non-profit organization or charity event and you'd like to be of service and give back to the community.

Remember Speaking for Free
GETS YOU A FEE

Here are some ways speaking pro bono can be beneficial and get you paid!

- It's a great way to travel and see the world. Focus on places you always wanted to visit or international events.

- Ask the event planner to pay for travel (hotel, plane, car, food reimbursement. dog care, ask if child or family member can travel too, etc.)

- Ask the event planner to introduce you to 3 colleagues via email or LinkedIn who also coordinate events. This can lead to instant paid bookings.

- Ask to secure a spot the following year for your speaking fee.

- Ask them to buy bulk copies of books (i.e. they may buy between 50 to 200 copies of your book)..

- Ask for the event to be recorded by a professional videographer and use this footage to book more events.

- If they have a large social media following ask for a shout-out on social media - think influencer marketing.

NEW SPEAKER

Chapter 16
New To Speaking? You Can Still Book Gigs!

"Your Voice Is A Gift, It Needs To Be Shared"
- Erika Talia McCarthy

New to Speaking?
YOU CAN STILL BOOK GIGS!

Are you a brand new speaker and worried that you won't be able to book public speaking engagements?

Although you haven't secured a speaking gig yet, all world-class speakers had to start somewhere. All speakers making $100,000 a year or more had their first speaking engagement once upon a time.

You may not have booked a speaking gig yet but you do have knowledge in an area that people will pay you to share.

Even if your first few speaking engagements are pro bono, remember what you learned in the previous chapter and understand that even free gigs can end up in large numbers of your products, books, and services being sold!

Even as a new public speaker, there are still ample opportunities to secure public speaking engagements. While experience may be a factor considered by event organizers, it is not the sole determining factor. As a new speaker, you can emphasize your unique perspective, fresh insights, and enthusiasm for sharing your knowledge.

Start by targeting smaller, local events and organizations that are open to showcasing emerging talent. Networking with fellow speakers, event organizers, and industry professionals can also lead to valuable connections and speaking opportunities.

Consider offering your speaking services at no charge or for an honorarium initially to gain exposure and build a portfolio.

You can ask for a videographer to record your speech in order to use that video to book more speaking engagements. Ask for the event to buy your books, products, and services in exchange for not receiving a speaking fee.

Ask for the event to pay for your plane, hotel, and car service especially if the event is in a city you've always wanted to visit.

Furthermore, ask the event coordinator if he/she can introduce you to three of their colleagues at the event, via email, or via LinkedIn who may need speakers. When you connect with these new event coordinators you can ask for a speaking fee.

Ask for written or video testimonials or use Talkadot to get feedback and testimonials.

As you gain experience and receive positive feedback, you can gradually transition to paid engagements.

However, if you are a new speaker you can still get paid! Ask for a speaking fee, don't sell yourself short. If the event has a budget you still deserve to be paid for your expertise.

If you do decide to speak pro bono, these are ideas on how to make sure you still receive some form of compensation and value outside of the many lives you are about to transform.

Furthermore, showcasing your expertise through content creation, such as writing articles or creating online videos, can help establish your credibility and attract speaking opportunities. With persistence, a well-crafted pitch, and a genuine passion for your subject matter, new public speakers can successfully secure public speaking engagements and begin their journey toward a thriving speaking career.

Your Voice Matters

You still have experience! Here are some ways to highlight your subject matter expertise!

- Did you help your company generate an additional $1 million?
- Do you have a wonderful marriage?
- Have you won employee of the month?
- Are you told you're organized and efficient?
- Have you successfully negotiated a raise?
- Are you always called to lead company meetings?
- Have you generated your first $100k in your business?

Key Takeaways!

WHAT ARE YOUR KEY TAKEAWAYS & ACTION PLAN?

Key Takeaways!

WHAT ARE YOUR KEY TAKEAWAYS & ACTION PLAN?

Key Takeaways!

WHAT ARE YOUR KEY TAKEAWAYS & ACTION PLAN?

Thank You

Chapter 17
Thank You!

"Your Voice Is A Gift, It Needs To Be Shared"
- Erika Talia McCarthy

Thank you so much for reading
**SPEAK NOW OR FOREVER HOLD YOUR SPEECH,
HOW TO BECOME AN IRRESISTIBLE & PAID SPEAKER!**

My truest and deepest desire for you is for you to have the ability to spread your message far and wide!

Don't stop until you get your message out there to the masses.

In conclusion, following your dreams of becoming a public speaker is a transformative journey that holds immense potential for personal growth, professional fulfillment, and making a lasting impact.

Throughout this book, we have explored the various aspects of pursuing a career in public speaking, from overcoming self-doubt to honing your speaking skills, finding opportunities, and navigating the industry.

We have emphasized the importance of authenticity, passion, and perseverance in carving your unique path as a speaker.

Remember, your voice and story have the power to inspire, educate, influence others, and transform lives.

By embracing your dreams and fearlessly stepping onto the stage, you open doors to unimaginable possibilities, connecting with diverse audiences and leaving a legacy through your words.

Embrace the journey, embrace your dreams, and let your voice soar as you embark on a fulfilling and impactful career as a public speaker. The world is waiting to hear your message.

I was in a hospital bed once listening to powerful speakers like yourself, speakers like you gave me the strength to walk again.

Who will you give legs to today?

We Can Assist You With The Following Done-For-You Services And More!

- Create your speaking bio
- Create your speaking video,
- Create a speaking page on your website
- Find in-person, virtual, and/or international speaking engagements
- Help you create your speaking proposals, titles, and descriptions
- Negotiate your speaking fees
- Ask for bulk copies of your books to be sold at the event
- Arrange for your speech to be recorded
- Get you booked on podcast interviews
- Ask for video or written testimonials
- Social Media Management
- Etsy Shop Set Up
- Digital Course Creation
- Copywriting and Email List Management
- And More!

Too busy to find and book your own speaking engagements? Let me help! Book a call below to learn how I can take tasks off of your plate so you can simply show up to your event and speak!

Book A Call

https://bit.ly/publicspeakersletschat

MySpeakersBoutique.com

Testimonials

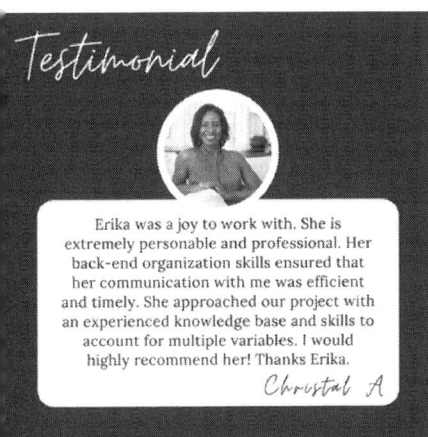

Testimonial

Erika was a joy to work with. She is extremely personable and professional. Her back-end organization skills ensured that her communication with me was efficient and timely. She approached our project with an experienced knowledge base and skills to account for multiple variables. I would highly recommend her! Thanks Erika.

Christal A

[Email From A Client-Partner After Booking Two Paid Speaking Engagements For Him]

"Great to hear!! Thank you so much! Excited :). I am avail on the 27th and excited to be a part!
Awesome about the potential for the following speaking engagements with them as well!
Very excited about this opportunity and our speaking future together!
Thank you, Erika!!"

-Alex W.

Testimonial

"Erika was always easy to reach, quick to respond, and easy to work with. I did land quite a few podcast bookings and got to meet others in the same field on the same mission; there was also an increase overall in book sales."

Jennifer G

Click To Watch A Testimonial Video

Find Your Next Speaking Engagement

SPEAKING DATABASE

WANT ACCESS TO MY PUBLIC SPEAKING DATABASE WITH 1000S OF EVENTS THAT NEED SPEAKERS & MY VIDEO TRAINING PORTAL WHERE I TEACH YOU HOW TO BOOK SPEAKING ENGAGEMENTS?

- 1200 Events currently in database for 2023 and 2024.//
- Easily Search by event type (virtual or in-person), location, application deadline, industry, etc.
- Training portal with step-by-step videos that teach you how to book engagements.

SCAN TO PREVIEW THE DATABASE

PAY & GAIN ACCESS TO THE DATABASE

Visit My Etsy Shop For More Public Speaking Resources!

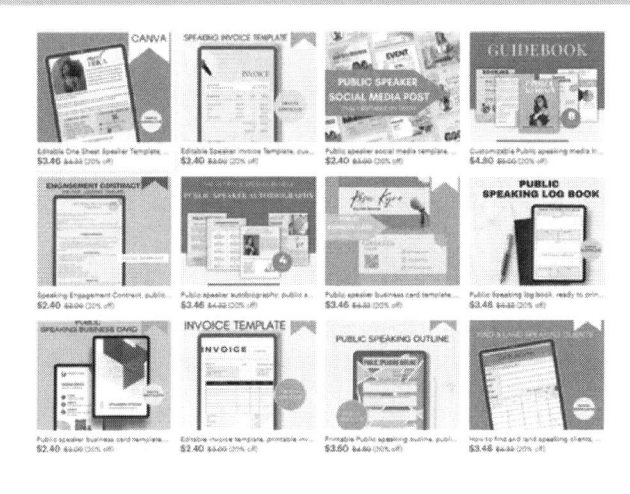

https://www.etsy.com/shop/MySpeakersBoutique

Made in the USA
Columbia, SC
20 June 2024